SPREAD YOUR HUSTLE

"THE BLUEPRINT TO FINANCIAL SUCCESS"

I0503242

HOW TO SPREAD YOUR HUSTLE & WIN WIN WIN!!!

100% PROVEN METHODS

BY: DAMION KING

Table of Contents

INTRODUCTION

Hi! I'm Damion King and I'd like to share with you a variety of 100% proven methods on how to spread your hustle. I have spent countless hours doing research and composing effective formulas that will allow you to obtain the financial stability that you've always wanted.

Despite the fact that most of us don't have the time or money to invest in the talents, hobbies or skills that could possibly get us where we desire to be financially, these methods will give you step by step guidelines on how to reach heights un-known within the corporate world. They say a journey of a thousand miles began with one step so take that step now and spread your hustle.

CHAPTER 1
HOW TO SPREAD YOR HUSTLE & WIN WIN WIN

If you want to be successful financially you must not limit yourself. You must be positive, creative, diverse and persistent. In today's world, especially with an un-stable economy, being able to spread your hustle is essential and very much beneficial.

Matter of fact, when you spread your hustle you're not subject to some of the stagnating obstacles such as check-to-check living, credit card debt, no or bad credit, lack of employment and welfare dependency just to name a few. Being an entrepreneur is not always easy, but neither is everyday life. However, I have composed a five step formula that will help you spread your hustle and win win win on any level. This method has been tested and proven many times by many different people in different industries and markets, and it actually works. Get started on the following steps so you too can spread your hustle and win win win.

STRENGTHEN YOUR MIND:

In order to spread your hustle you must first strengthen your mind by obtaining enlightenment on a particular industry or market of choice. Then you must think positive and use your imagination to explore and discover. We can only get out of life what we can imagine, so the things we see in our minds we tend to materialize through our actions.

This process allows you to condition your mind and focus on doing whatever is necessary to help you spread your hustle on every level possible. Start strengthening your mind now through a variety of business literature for the enlightenment you need or desire to make progress and grow.

BROADEN YOUR HORIZONS:

This step is very important when spreading your hustle. There are several ways to broaden your horizons such as reading and studying business literature, attending seminars and conventions, blending your energy with others within different social groups who are business oriented, and doing a research analysis on different industries and/or markets you desire to do business in.

It's a known fact that knowledge/information is power. Not jus in the business world, but in life in general so broaden your horizons on every level as much as possible as often as you can.

COMPOSE YOUR STRATEGY:

A strategy is a method of operation. It consist of making preparations to put forth an effort to accomplish your task, which means you are brain storming, taking notes and creating a process of order in which things will be done. This is where you create your plan and determine how it will be executed. Composing your strategy is very beneficial and shows professionalism.

EXERCISING YOUR POTENTIAL:

Exercising your potential is very similar to composing your strategy, but not the same. When exercising your potential you are carrying out the plan that you have composed. For example, where are you going to obtain capital for equipment and materials, what positioning statement will you use to draw customers to you and away from competitors, how to advertise/promote the business, when to actually open the business and things of the like. Everyone must have an effective and diverse strategy that will further their plans and spread their hustle.

SPREAD YOUR HUSTLE:

This last step is not easy, but it's fun because by this time you would have realized that you are making progress. When spreading your hustle you must execute your plan by using the strategy you composed. Once the wheels are turning and spreading your hustle has become fruitful reality. Stay focused, work hard, manage and invest your money wisely. Then repeat all five steps.

This five step formula is guaranteed to help you spread your hustle and win win win. Don't wait until tomorrow to get started…….spread your hustle today!

CHAPTER 2

HOW TO GET A TRIPLE A-1 CREDIT RATING IN 45 TO 60 DAYS

Sometimes we have trouble obtaining things such as houses, cars or other necessities because we have no or bad credit for lack of making wiser decisions, and we find ourselves trying to cut through the red tape of improving our credit score. Fortunately, I have come up with a way to get a triple A-1 credit rating in 45 to 60 days that has been over looked for decades. All you have to do is follow the instructions below.

Take $500 to the bank (any bank of choice) and open a savings account. Next, wait three days to make sure your account has been posted and then apply for a $500 loan. You can offer to use your savings account as collateral (it's a risk free loan for the bank, but make sure the bank offers you a premium).

Now you have $500 in the bank drawing interest and $500 in your pocket. (The $500 in savings account will be frozen). Take the $500 in your pocket to a second bank and open up another savings account. Three days later go back to the second bank and apply for a $500 loan. Once again offer to use your savings account at second bank as collateral (this is a risk free loan for the bank) Now you have $500 drawing interest in savings account, which will be frozen and you have $500 in your pocket. Repeat this same process with at least three other banks. (a total of five banks being used).

After you have opened savings account at five different banks and obtained loans at each bank, take $500 loan from last bank (fifth bank) and go open up a checking account at any bank of choice three days later. Next, start writing payment checks! When writing payment checks make sure you pay one full month's payment at each bank that you got a loan from. One week later, make another payment to each of the same five banks. Continue this same process until loans from all five banks are paid off,

At this rate or pace you will have all loans paid off in 45 to 60! With each payment an equal amount of the money will be un-frozen in the savings account. You can then take this money (in savings account) and place it in your checking account as you go along. After three early payments the bank will clear you for future signature loans at their bank and will give you a triple A-1 credit rating to any bureau checking your credit rating!!!

Don't miss out on this opportunity to experience the financial stability you have envisioned for years!!!

"HELPFUL HINTS YOU MAY EMPLOY WHILE WORKING THIS PLAN"

Always take your savings account book with you when applying for a loan since you may have to surrender it to loan officer at bank.

Always try to get a nine month payback plan for each loan even though you will pay them back much sooner.

<u>**USE THESE HELPFUL HINTS!!!!!!!!**</u>

BONUS EDITION:
HOW TO GET A PERSONAL LOAN FOR $25,000

Go to the bank and apply for a personal loan! Do not tell loan officer you are borrowing money to finance a business!!! Tell the loan officer that the money will be used for home improvement or something that would require an appreciable sum of money such as you are asking for. (This could not be said to be illegal since you could have changed your mind about what to do with the money once you received the loan.) If you need a loan as soon as possible and have not yet obtained a triple A-1 credit rating you may need a co-signer to get the loan.

FOLLOW THESE FIVE STEPS

1. Go to the five banks where you have established yourself and get a "personal loan application" from each bank.

2. Fill out each application requesting a $5,000 personal loan.

3. Take applications to the banks you got them from all in the same day.

4. If you are established (Good credit/Triple A-1 credit rating) you will receive the loan.

5. Take the money and make your investment….but invest wisely! This loan must be paid back and it must be paid back on time! If not you will not keep the triple A-1 credit rating you worked so hard to obtain!

Having good credit is a beneficial privilege that we all should want to have, keep and put to use which means we must appreciate and maintain an acceptable credit score or rating at all times! If you have no or bad credit now is the time to change that status with a triple A-1 credit rating! Don't miss out!!!

CHAPTER 3
HOW TO START A SUCCESSFUL BUSINESS

Owing a successful business is one thing that every business owner would love to experience. Despite the fact that starting a successful business is tough, applying solid principals will help you increase your chances of success.

There are five key areas that you should focus on when starting a business which includes conducting an effective research of the market, creating an effective marketing plan, financing your business, knowing how to manage your cash flow and staying focused on being committed.

It is very essential to develop a plan of action before you began doing business. If you read, understand, learn and apply the five steps that you will read in this chapter, you will most likely be successful. Take a look at the five steps below and began preparing to start your own successful business.

RESEARCHING THE MARKET:

When starting a successful business doing effective and extensive research is very important. You could depend on the bits of information or opinions you get from your family or friends, but I encourage you to hire a professional research firm to do a market analysis for you. This way you will be able to see a clearer picture of what's going on in a particular market and obtain the valuable information you need to do business effectively and successfully in that market. Also, I encourage you to use the internet. The internet can provide you with a variety of information sources concerning any market or industry.

CREATING AN EFFECTIVE MARKETING PLAN:

After you decide to start your business getting the word out about your company is mandatory, even if your marketing budget is small. There are cost effective ways to attract consumers and make every penny count. However, marketing is very critical for any business and determines the amount of cash flow. When creating an effective marketing plan you may need to apply the 5 P's of marketing, which are **product, place**, **price, promotion and positioning** statement. You can use media outlets to market your business to the public as well as flyers, grand opening event and word of mouth.

FINANCING YOUR BUSINESS:

Insufficient funds are one of the main reasons a business fails. Whether your business is jus starting or on the verge of growing you should know the many different ways to finance your business. Most business owners try not to put all their personal money at risk, which is a good tactic.

However, they have been known to get the necessary financing from venture capitalist, angel investors, banks or even friends and family, In any case, having a business plan is a must which includes realistic revenues and market projections as well as a solid business model.

KNOWING HOW TO MANAGE YOUR CASH FLOW:

Your cash flow is the capital that comes into your business from consumers patronizing your business. This capital must be recorded, accounted for and utilized wisely to ensure the success of the business. You should structure a plan that will help you keep track of who handles the management of the company's cash flow and what it's spent on. Knowing how to manage your company's cash flow will help you keep a low overhead and a substantial amount of inventory.

STAYING FOCUSED ON YOUR COMMITMENT:

Being able to constantly be committed is a must when starting and running your own business. You must focus on ways to create a strategy that will allow you to exceed consumer's expectations. Your commitment must be your business culture and the essence of your overall business strategy. I think your business is much more than goods and services. A business should help make consumers lives better and provide solutions to problems. Staying focused on customer service is essential to having a successful business.

These five steps will help you put your start-up plans into action and start a successful business. Time is money and we can't afford to waste either of the two! Start your successful business now!!!

For more info contact The Small Business Administration office in your state or go online at www.sba.gov. They provide free information on how to start your own business.

CHAPTER 4
HOW TO FORM YOUR LIMITED LIABILITY COMPANY:

The limited liability company is a very popular business structure due to its diversity and flexibility. It acts as its own person and is a separate entity that's distinct from its owners. It can conduct business, establish credit, incur liabilities, acquire assets and buy, sale or trade just as you can, but your personal assets are not at risk. You only risk what you invest into the company itself. This business structure is very easy to form and has been used by corporate executives, government officials and even ex-cons among others.

This section will give you step by step insight on how to form your limited liability company. Don't wait any longer, turn the page and get started now! This is an effective and beneficial way to spread your hustle and reach financial success!

NAME RESERVATION:

Once you have chosen a name for your business you should reserve that name which will be included in your articles of organization when filing your limited liability company. In case your chosen name for your business is not available you should have other alternative names to use in place of the first name you chose.

The name of your business should be unregistered, that is, no other business in the state you are filing your business in is already using the name or a similar name. Each state has different rules as to words that can or can not be used in your business name.

You can select a name that will help consumers identify the type of product or services your business provides. To reserve your business name contact the secretary of state's office in your incorporation state or an incorporation service company to find out if it's available or not.

If your business will be doing business in more than one state, consider reserving your name in every state where you will be doing business prior to filing your limited liability company in any state. However, if the name you choose is not available in another state you will have to choose another name before you can do business in that state. There will be a onetime fee to reserve your business name.

SELECT YOUR BUSINESS STRUCTURE:

There are several business structures to choose from which includes sole proprietorship, c-corporation, s-corporation, partnership and Limited Liability Company. Here is where you choose which business structure is appropriate for you. In this case it's Limited Liability Company. Below are each business structure and their advantages & disadvantages.

> ***SOLE PROPRIETORSHIP:*** Simple and inexpensive to create and operate. Owner reports profit or loss on personal tax return. Owner personally liable for business debts. Not a separate entity.

> ***C-CORPORATION:*** Clients have less risk from government audits. Owners have limited personal liability for business debts. Owners can deduct fringe benefits as business expense; Owners can split corporate profit among owners and corporation, paying lower overall tax rate. It's more expensive to create and operate than sole proprietorship or partnership, Double taxation threat because the corporation is a separate taxable entity has no beneficial employment tax treatment.

S-CORPORATION: Clients have less risk from government audits, owners have limited personal liability for business debts, owners can use corporate losses to offset income from other status, owners can save on employment taxes by taking distributions instead of salary, It's more expensive to create and operate than sole proprietorship and fringe benefits for shareholders are limited. There can only be seventy five shareholders and you don't pay self employment tax.

PARTNERSHIP: Simple and inexpensive to create and operate, owners report profit or loss on personal tax returns, owners are personally liable for business debts, two or more owners are required and there is no beneficial employment tax treatment.

LIMITED LIABILITY COMPANY: Owners have limited liability for business debts if they participate in management, profit and loss can be allocated differently than ownership interest and there's no beneficial employment tax.

TRADEMARK/PATENT REGISTRATION:

Apply for trademark or patent registration to protect your assets. You trademark your company name and/or logo to distinguish your company from another company, and prevent other's from using them. For more info go online to www.uspto.gov

EMPLOYER IDENTIFICATION NUMBER:

Once you file your paperwork with the secretary of state office you must apply for a federal or state E.I.N.# (Employer Identification Number). One will be needed for tax purposes. For more info go online to **www.irs.gov**

BUSINESS LIECENSE:

Go apply for a business license needed for whatever type of business you are starting. For more info go online to **www.sba.gov**

BUSINESS INSURANCE:

Go apply for workers compensation and any other type of insurance needed through private carriers. (Workers compensation is required in certain states when a business has three or more employees regardless of the hours they work). For more info go online to **www.sba.gov**

REGISTERED AGENT:

State laws require that you have an "agent" of the limited liability company who is responsible for receiving and forwarding vital legal and tax documents. The designated registered agent must be a resident of the state of corporation or L.L.C formation. The address of the agent must be a physical address, not a P.O Box, and it must be open during all normal business hours. A registered agent serves as a conduit for managing ongoing legal requirements associated with your company.

Your agent receives official state and federal mail, such as tax forms and annual report notices. The agent may also be served with legal papers (notice of litigation) if a lawsuit is filed against the L.L.C. The person designated to be the registered agent may or may not be affiliated with your limited liability company. The agent may be an employee, officer, director or shareholder of corporation, or may be a third person/party. You may serve as your own agent with your principal office address as the registered agent address. However, most business owners choose a third party to act in this capacity. For more info go online to **www.sba.gov**

LEGAL ASSISTANCE:

You must consult with a business lawyers as well as a certified public accountant to complete the formation of your limited liability company for tax purposes. Laws and other regulations can be very complex so make sure you have legal assistance to help you navigate the process.

File your limited liability company now and spread your hustle like never before! Financial success is right around the corner!!! For more info on how to form your own limited liability companies go online to **www.sba.gov**

CHAPTER 5

HOW TO MAKE TAX FREE MONEY LEGALLY AFTER FORMING YOUR C-CORPORATION:

Corporations are entities that are separate from their owners. This means that corporate shareholders are protected from liability for the company's debts. If a business gets into serious financial trouble, the law prevents creditors from coming after shareholders assets, as long as that debt was not personally guaranteed. Shareholders have only the money they put into the company to lose.

A corporation can raise money directly through the sale of stock and bond offerings, and can borrow from commercial sources, using corporate assets to secure a loan.

Forming a corporation helps business owners save on self-employment taxes. Self-employed owners pay 15.3% of their total earnings to cover Medicare and social security obligations.

Contrast this with the business owner who forms a corporation who pays self-employment taxes only on that portion of profit that is paid out as salary. But S corporations' dividends are not subject to self-employment tax.

The main advantage of a C-Corporation (a general corporation) is that it has an unlimited number of shareholders or classes of stock. A C-Corporation is appropriate for companies that plan to have more than more than thirty stockholders or large public stock offerings, but smaller companies choose this business structure also. However, there is one major disadvantage and that is all_profits are subject to double taxation. (Corporate income is taxed and the dividends paid to each stockholder are taxed as part of their income).

It is possible to get cash by forming a corporation and selling shares of stock. In writing the charter for the corporation you can authorize an issue of one million shares of stock at no par value. The money you get from the sale of shares of stock is interest free, doesn't have to be paid back, pays your salary and is tax free! This can make you incredibly successful financially! Read the example below.

After forming a corporation, an issue of one million shares is authorized. You keep 400,000 shares of the stock for yourself. Then take 300,000 shares of stock and set them to the side for sale to the public at $1.00 per share. The other remaining 300,000 shares of stock should remain with your company for sale to the public at a later date.

Next, put 80,000 shares of the 300,000 shares of stock up for sale to the public. It is very probable that a "brokerage firm" has heard of your corporation by now.

They will offer to sale your shares of stock for you at a 20% commission. So almost immediately you have risen over $130,000! (Which means, the 80,000 shares, were sold at $2.00 per share).

Later when your corporation starts doing business and becomes familiar to the public, more people will start to become interested in your corporation and wish to buy shares of stock in your company. As this takes place the value of your stock will rise steadily!

One day when you visit your stock broker you will find out your company stock will be up to about $4.00 per share. Suddenly you will remember that you own 400,000 shares of company stock and that they are now worth $4.00 per share! Almost overnight your net worth has rocketed to $1,600,000.00 (one point six million dollars).

Also, you still have the money from the sale of the original 300,000 shares of stock that you set aside to sale to the public at a later date.(you should have made $240,000 from selling those shares at $1.00 per share).

All monies made from the sales of shares of stock should be used to grow and market your company! This is not just wishful thinking! Similar and even more spectacular cases occur in the business world around us and we never know how they got off the ground!

However, there is a draw back here. Yes, of course you will need legal assistance from a lawyer and certified public accountant since the securities & exchange commission (sec) regulations are so complex!!

Your company must be registered with or through the (sec) securities & exchange commission to go public in most cases. For more info go online to www.sba.gov or www.score.org

BONUS EDITION:
PENNY STOCKS

Yes, of course there is a way to go public without registering your company with the securities & exchange commission!

If you price your company stock at a dime each share (10 cents per share) and keep the total selling price of the shares under $50,000 you do not need the (sec) securities & exchange commission when going public.

The shares are then called "Penny Stocks"!

To sale this stock you would need to issue "100 share lots" and start in your area, trading in your area. (Flea markets, fairs, and similar places might be good places to start).

Try to get all the publicity you can get!

Two important things you should know about the money you earn from the sale of penny stocks is that it's interest free, it never has to be paid back !!!

This "100% PROVEN METHOD" has been used for many years by people of all races and professions including ex-cons! Do not wait any longer! Spread your hustle and make millions now!!!

For more info go online to www.sba.gov or www.score.org

CHAPTER 6
HOW TO GROW YOUR COMPANY WITH THE 5 P'S OF MARKETING

Every business of any kind must use some sort of marketing tool or strategy to sale their product or service to consumers. If not, the business will go out of business immediately! However, some business owners use traditional tactics while others use new and creative ways that has never before been seen or heard of.

If I had a choice between traditional tactics and the new and creative ways to grow my business effectively I would use traditional tactics, which are called "The 5 P's Of Marketing" in the corporate world.

This marketing strategy is very simple, effective and profitable. It has been used by many business owners in different industries and markets, and continues to be "the numbcr one marketing strategy" used to grow small businesses!

This marketing strategy, if used correctly, will help you obtain the financial success you've always desired no matter the product or service you are providing for the public.

This 100% Proven Method is one of a kind and it actually works! Check out the five step formula below.

THE 5 P'S OF MARKETING

PRODUCT: your product or service must be new, unique or different. It must be a necessity of some kind and not a fad. (Fads go away sooner or later). Your product or service must be appealing to the consumer.

PLACE: Location is very important to consumers. Your product or service must be easy to get to or obtain. (Accessible by public transportation as well as personal transportation). It must be in a newly developed area (residential or commercial, depending on product or service) or in highly frequented area such as busy intersection or plaza.

PRICE: How much your product or service cost will make you or break you. Your prices must be the same as competitors or lower, but reasonable and affordable at the same time. Your prices must be convenient for consumers.

PROMOTION: If you don't promote or advertise your product or service it will not sale! Promotion is sometimes very expensive. But it's also very effective. You must promote your product or service in ways that will reach the consumers ears and eyes. For example, you can use radio, TV, internet, flyers, business cards, newspapers, magazines, parties and word of mouth to promote your product or services effectively.

POSITIONING STATEMENT: Every business must have a gimmick! It may be a motto or slogan of some kind that draws the consumer to your company and away from competitors. Something that allows your consumers to relate to what you are offering. You have to give to receive so you must use clearance sales, buy 2 get 1 free deal, free food or a contest or raffle of some kind to grab and hold the attention of the consumers.

Once you began using this 100% PROVEN METHOD on how to grow your business you will appreciate the power and ability of The 5 P's Of Marketing. DO NOT LOSE OR MIS-USE THIS, BUT USE THIS!!! For more info go online to www.sba.gov or www.score.org

CHAPTER 7

HOW TO START A COMMERCIAL CLEANING COMPANY FOR UNDER $1,000

When choosing a business name you want to choose one that is catchy, but professional. Once you have chosen a name for your commercial cleaning company you should develop a logo for your company that reflects the name you chose.

There are certain requirements and/or business license that are needed as well as insurance. You will need to call your city hall or state government as well as an insurance company about getting your commercial cleaning company bonded.

Next you should have some business cards made with your company name, logo, and contact information and if your company is bonded you should have that information on the business card also.

You can get business cards and fliers printed up through a variety of companies to advertise and promote your commercial cleaning company to potential clients.

Then you should develop a hourly rate that is reasonable, but competitive with other cleaning companies in the area. (You can call other cleaning companies to inquire about their rates).

Of course cleaning supplies and materials are needed so I would suggest that you go to a Dollar Tree store to get the basic cleaning supplies.

However, some clients may provide their own cleaning supplies, but it is highly recommended that you have your own cleaning supplies and material. Initially, when just starting your commercial cleaning company you can use your home phone or cell phone line until you can get a separate phone line for your company.

This is where you should start advertising your company services using forms of free advertising such as fliers that include your company name, logo, prices, and contact information.

You should then put them in high traffic areas such as libraries, supermarkets, restaurants and places of the like. Also spread the word that you are in business because word of mouth is a great form of promoting.

You can also put an ad in the classified section of your local newspaper.

These are inexpensive ways to advertise and promote your cleaning company. Research and seek small commercial cleaning jobs. Market your company and do the work yourself.

That way you will know how long it takes to complete a job, which cleaning method to use and what supplies are needed.

I encourage you to read literature and listen to audio about how to start your own commercial cleaning company as well as getting the proper janitorial training. Even though you are just starting you should try to be flexible with your pricing for projects.

It's good to take notes on your first few jobs to keep track of what equipment and supplies is needed.

You can use this data to bid on other commercial cleaning jobs and you can also work as a sub-contractor by doing cleaning jobs for bigger commercial cleaning companies.

MAKE GOING GREEN AN OPTION FOR YOUR COMPANY

Today there is an eco-friendly demand and if you use eco friendly products as well as methods you can make a difference. If you decide to go green you should mention that when advertising your company to separate your company from among the rest.

A commercial cleaning company consists of task such as carpet cleaning, window cleaning, vacuuming, cleaning offices and commercial buildings.

Most likely a commercial cleaning company's contract will stipulate that you receive payment monthly or bi-weekly after services has been rendered.

Janitorial cleaning that is done during the day includes dusting, window cleaning, re-filling soap dispensers, emptying garbage containers, vacuuming, sweeping and waxing floors.

At night and after business hours cleaning such as mopping, carpet shampooing, and waxing are done. If the jobs are small they can be done with just one or two people.

Normally, when just starting a commercial cleaning company you can start out using regular household cleaning supplies and equipment.

The basic household cleaning supplies and equipment does not cost much.

However, if you don't use Dollar Tree there are wholesalers who sell inexpensive commercial cleaning supplies and equipment in bulk so that you save on your investment.

It is also a great idea to search sites like EBay and Craig's List for bargains on cleaning supplies and equipment as well.

THINGS YOU WILL NEED TO GET STARTED

1. Name for your company
2. Business cards
3. Fliers

4. Cleaning supplies and equipment

5. Company telephone line

6. Vehicle

CLEANING SUPPLIES AND EQUIPMENT TO USE

1. Commercial Vacuum Cleaner

2. Dust Mops

3. Brooms

4. Mops

5. Bleach

6. Disinfectant (all-purpose cleaners)

7. Trash Bags (tall kitchen & outdoor)

8. Buckets

9. Latex Gloves

10. Liquid Hand Soap

11. Dust Pan

12. Carpet Shampoo

13. Push Brooms

14. Brown Paper Towels (multi-fold towels & roll towels)

15. Spray Bottles

16. Hand Sanitizer

17. Dust cloths

18. Waste Container (55 Gallon)

I have given you a 100% Proven Method on how to start your commercial cleaning company for under $1,000. Don't waste any more time! Get started today!